Sisters by Algernon Charles Swinburne

A TRAGEDY

Algernon Charles Swinburne was born on April 5th, 1837, in London, into a wealthy Northumbrian family. He was educated at Eton and at Balliol College, Oxford, but did not complete a degree.

In 1860 Swinburne published two verse dramas but achieved his first literary success in 1865 with Atalanta in Calydon, written in the form of classical Greek tragedy. The following year "Poems and Ballads" brought him instant notoriety. He was now identified with "indecent" themes and the precept of art for art's sake.

Although he produced much after this success in general his popularity and critical reputation declined. The most important qualities of Swinburne's work are an intense lyricism, his intricately extended and evocative imagery, metrical virtuosity, rich use of assonance and alliteration, and bold, complex rhythms.

Swinburne's physical appearance was small, frail, and plagued by several other oddities of physique and temperament. Throughout the 1860s and 1870s he drank excessively and was prone to accidents that often left him bruised, bloody, or unconscious. Until his forties he suffered intermittent physical collapses that necessitated removal to his parents' home while he recovered.

Throughout his career Swinburne also published literary criticism of great worth. His deep knowledge of world literatures contributed to a critical style rich in quotation, allusion, and comparison. He is particularly noted for discerning studies of Elizabethan dramatists and of many English and French poets and novelists As well he was a noted essayist and wrote two novels.

In 1879, Swinburne's friend and literary agent, Theodore Watts-Dunton, intervened during a time when Swinburne was dangerously ill. Watts-Dunton isolated Swinburne at a suburban home in Putney and gradually weaned him from alcohol, former companions and many other habits as well.

Much of his poetry in this period may be inferior but some individual poems are exceptional; "By the North Sea," "Evening on the Broads," "A Nympholept," "The Lake of Gaube," and "Neap-Tide."

Swinburne lived another thirty years with Watts-Dunton. He denied Swinburne's friends access to him, controlled the poet's money, and restricted his activities. It is often quoted that 'he saved the man but killed the poet'.

Swinburne died on April 10th, 1909 at the age of seventy-two.

Index of Contents

TO THE LADY MARY GORDON

THIS PLAY IS GRATEFULLY INSCRIBED BY HER AFFECTIONATE NEPHEW

DEDICATION.

I.

Between the sea-cliffs and the sea there sleeps
A garden walled about with woodland, fair
As dreams that die or days that memory keeps
Alive in holier light and lovelier air
Than clothed them round long since and blessed
them there

With less benignant blessing, set less fast
For seal on spirit and sense, than time has cast
For all time on the dead and deathless past.

II.

Beneath the trellised flowers the flowers that shine
And lighten all the lustrous length of way
From terrace up to terrace bear me sign
And keep me record how no word could say
What perfect pleasure of how pure a da>'

A child's remembrance or a child's delight
Drank deep in dreams of, or in present sight
Exulted as the sunrise in its might.

III.

The shadowed lawns, the shadowing pines, the ways
That wind and wander through a world of dowers,
The radiant orchard where the glad sun's gaze
Dwells, and makes most of all his happiest hours,
The field that laughs beneath the cliff that towers,
The splendour of the slumber that enthralls
With sunbright peace the world within their walls,
Are symbols yet of years that love recalls.

IV.

But scarce the sovereign symbol of the sea,
That clasps about the loveliest land alive
With loveliness more wonderful, may be
Fit sign to show what radiant dreams survive
Of suns that set not with the years that drive
Like mists before the blast of dawn, but still
Through clouds and gusts of change that chafe and chill
Lift up the light that mocks their wrathful will.

V.

A light unshaken of the wind of time
That laughs upon the thunder and the threat
Of years that thicken and of clouds that climb
To put the stars out that they see not set,
And bid sweet memory's rapturous faith forget.
But not the lightning shafts of change can slay
The life of light that dies not with the day,
The glad live past that cannot pass away.

VI.

The many-coloured joys of dawn and noon
That lit with love a child's life and a boy's,
And kept a man's in concord and in tune
With lifelong music of memorial joys
Where thought held life and dream in equipoise,

Even now make child and boy and man seem one.
And days that dawned beneath the last year's sun
As days that even ere childhood died were done.

VII.

The sun to sport in and the cliffs to scale,
The sea to clasp and wrestle with, till breath
For rapture more than weariness would fail,
All-golden gifts of dawn, whose record saith
That time nor change may turn their life to death,
lave not in loving thought alone, though there
The life they live be lovelier than they were
When clothed in present light and actual air.

VIII.

Sun, moon, and stars behold the land and sea
No less than ever lovely, bright as hope
Could hover, or as happiness can be:
Fair as of old the lawns to sunward slope,
The fields to seaward slant and close and ope:
But where of old from strong and sleepless wells
The exulting fountains fed their shapely shells,
Where light once dwelt in water, dust now dwells.

IX.

The springs of earth may slacken, and the sun
Find no more laughing lustre to relume
Where once the sunlight and the spring seemed one;
But not on heart or soul may time or doom
Cast aught of drought or lower with aught of gloom
If past and future, hope and memory, be
Ringed round about with love, fast bound and free,
As all the world is girdled with the sea.

PERSONS REPRESENTED
Sir Francis Dilston.
Sir Arthur Clavering.
Frank Dilston, son to Sir Francis.
Reginald Clavering, cousin to Sir Arthur.
Anne Dilston   } twin-sister's and co-heiresses, formerly wards

Mabel Dilston   } of Sir Francis.

SCENE

Clavering Hall, Northumberland.

TIME
1816.

CHARACTERS IN THE INTERLUDE
Alvise Vivarini, represented by Reginald Clavering.
Calasso Galassi, represented by Frank Dilston.
Beatrice Signorelli, represented by Mabel Dilston.
Francesca Mariani, , represented by Anne Dilston.

ACT I

SCENE I. — A Morning Room

ANNE and **MABEL.**

ANNE
April again, and not a word of war.
Last year, and not a year ago, it was
That we sat wondering when good news would come.

MABEL
And had not heard or learnt in lesson-books
If such a place there was as Waterloo.
And never dreamed that—

ANNE
Well?

MABEL
That it would be
So soon for ever such a name for us
As Blenheim or Trafalgar.

ANNE
No. For us?
We don't remember Blenheim — and we had
No cousin wounded at Trafalgar. Still,

If Redgie had been old enough to serve

MABEL
I wish he had chosen the navy.

ANNE
And come home
Unhurt?

MABEL
No; I forgot. Of course he might
Have died like Nelson — and gone home with him.

ANNE
Home? Reginald's not quite so tired of life,
I fancy, though he frets at being kept in,
As to look up— outside this world — for home.

MABEL
No.

ANNE
Will you tell me — but you will not — me,
Even

MABEL
What? Anything I can I will.

ANNE
Perhaps you cannot — what he said to you
Yesterday?

MABEL
When?

ANNE
You will not now, I know.

MABEL
Where?

ANNE
When and where? If you must needs be told,
At nine last evening in the library.

MABEL
Nothing— but what I meant to tell you.

ANNE
Yes?
You meant to tell me that he said, my dear,
What?

MABEL
Anne!

ANNE
You thought I knew?

MABEL
I thought I must
Have said it without speaking.

ANNE
Reginald!
And so you really mean to love the boy
You played with, rode with, climbed with, laughed at, made
Your tempter — and your scapegoat — when you chose
To ride forbidden horses, and break bounds
On days forbidden? Love! Of course you like—
And then how can you love him?

MABEL
Is dislike
Mother of love? Then you — to judge by signs —
Must love Frank Dilston dearly.

ANNE
So I might,
If — if I did not hate him.

MABEL
Then you do.
I'm glad. I always liked him.

ANNE
What has he
Done, that a woman— or a girl — should like
Him?

MABEL
Need a man — or boy— do anything
More than be true and bright and kind and brave
And try to make you like him?

ANNE

He should not try.
That spoils all

MABEL
I'll tell him not to try.

[Enter **REGINALD CLAVERING** and **FRANK DILSTON**.

ANNE
Redgie! You've not been riding?

REGINALD
Have I, Frank?

FRANK
You'd have me tell a lie to get you off?

ANNE
You stupid pair of schoolboys! Really, Frank,
You should not let him.

FRANK
I can't lick him, Anne;
We two—or you alone — might manage.

ANNE
Why,
The grooms must know he should not mount a horse
Yet.

REGINALD
Would you have me never ride again
Because last year I got a fall?

ANNE
Appeal
To Mabel

REGINALD
She was always hard on me.

MABEL
Always.

ANNE
You mean that I encouraged you
To risk your neck when we were girl and boy?
Make him sit down, Frank.

REGINALD
There. And now well talk
Of something — not of nothing.

ANNE
Of your play?

REGINALD
That's ready. How about your stage?

ANNE
But is it
Indeed?

REGINALD
It's just one little act, you know —
Enough for four and not too much, I hope,
To get by heart in half a pair of days.

ANNE
In one day? No; I am slow at learning verse —
Even if my part were shorter than the rest.

REGINALD
It is.

ANNE
Ah! Thank you.

FRANK
Mabel's I have read.
It's longer.

MABEL
As the whole affair is short,
It cannot be much longer. You should rest,
Redgie. Come out and feed the pheasants, Anne,

[Exeunt **ANNE** and **MABEL**.

REGINALD
How like old times it is, when we came back
From Eton! You remember, Frank, we played
—What was it?—once.

FRANK
'What was it?' There's no such play.

There's 'What you will': perhaps we played
'Twelfth Night'
In frocks and jackets. Might we now not play
'Love's Labour's Lost'?

REGINALD
'A Midsummer Night's Dream':
I know, because I played Lysander — you
Demetrius.

FRANK
How the female parts were cast
You don't remember?

REGINALD
Helena was Anne,
I think, and Hermia Mabel.

FRANK
Change the names.

REGINALD
Ah, yes. All friends from more than twelve miles round
Came in to our Yuletide gathering through the snows.
How quick and bright Anne's acting was! you two
Bore off the palms all round: Mabel and I
Were somewhere short of nowhere.

FRANK
Will you now
Retaliate? She and you were plotting this,
Must we suppose, last evening?

REGINALD
She and I,
Frank? We should make but poor conspirators.

FRANK
I hope so, and I think so. Seriously,
May not I ask—?

REGINALD
If she and I are friends?
Surely a man may ask and answer that,
If—as you do— 'he knows it. If you mean
More— I would hardly tell a brother this,
Who had not been so close a friend of mine '
Always, and had no right to ask me this —

No.

FRANK
Then she does not think — she has no cause-
She cannot think you love her?

REGINALD
Can I tell?
But this I can tell — she shall never come
To think or dream I do, and vex herself,
By any base and foolish fault of mine.

FRANK
But if she loves you, Redgie?

REGINALD
No, my boy.
She does not. Come, we need not talk of that.
I think mock-modesty a mincing lie—
The dirtiest form of self-conceit that is,
Quite, and in either sense the vainest. You
She may not love just yet— but me, I know,
She never will I ought to say 'Thank God,'
Being poor, and knowing myself unworthy her
—A younger son's son, with a closed career
Should peace prove now as stable as it looks —
If I on my side loved her as I should
And if I knew she would be, as I fear —
No, hope she will, happier with you than me.
I can't do that, quite; if I could, and did,
I should be just a little less unfit
To dream that she could love me — which I don't.

FRANK
You don't mean that you want me—

REGINALD
I do mean
I want her to be happy: as for you,
If I don't want you to be miserable
It only shows I am not quite a cur.

FRANK
You never were: but if you meant me well,
What made you go campaigning and come back
A hero?

REGINALD

Six months' service! Don't you be
A fool — or flatterer.

FRANK
Still, you have (worse luck!)
Such heavy odds—a wound, and Waterloo!

REGINALD
If I — or you— had lost an eye or arm,
That wouldn't make us Nelsons.

FRANK
Something like.

REGINALD
Well, you can do that in the hunting-field.

FRANK
I wish I had you in the playing fields
Again.

REGINALD
We can't just settle it with fists.
But, if you asked me as of course you don't
And won't, what she and I were talking of
Last evening, I could tell you - and I will.
I asked her if she thought it possible
That two such baby friends and playfellows
As she and Anne had been with you and me
Could, when grown-up, be serious lovers.

FRANK
Well—
Was that not making love to her? And what
Did she say?

REGINALD
Hardly. No. Certainly not.

FRANK
And then?

REGINALD
The bell rang, and we went to dress
For dinner.

FRANK
What did she say— if she did —

To make you ask her that?

REGINALD
Something she did—
At least, I thought so — like a fool. And now
We'll talk no more about it. Mind you, Frank,
I didn't— could I possibly?— forget
That just because I love her— more than you
I won't say— she must never dream I do
If I can help it.

FRANK
Then, in heaven's name, why
Say what you say you did?

REGINALD
Don't fret yourself.
No harm was meant or done. But if she does
Love you — if you can win her — as I think
(There!) — you're the happiest fellow ever born.

FRANK
And you're the best, Redgie. By Jove! she ought
To love you, if she knew how you love her.

REGINALD
And that, please God, she never will. When you
And she are married, if you tell her so,
You'll play the traitor, not to me but her —
Make her unhappy for the minute. Don't.
She would be sorrier than I'm worth, you know,
To think of any sorrow not her own
And given by her unconsciously. She had
Always the sweetest heart a girl could have.
'Sweet heart'! she might have been the first girl born
Whose lover ever called her by the name.

FRANK
Redgie, I don't know what to say to you.

REGINALD
Say nothing. Talk about our play.

FRANK
Your play!
We are like to play, it seems, without a stage,
Another, and a sadder.

REGINALD
Don't be sure.
My play is highly tragic. Italy,
Steel, poison, shipwreck—

FRANK
One you made at school,
Is it? I know what those were.

REGINALD
Wait and see.

[Enter **SIR FRANCIS DILSTON**.

SIR FRANCIS
Well, Frank, —how are you, Reginald? — you let
Mabel go out— and unattended?

FRANK
Come,
Father, you would not have me (think how she
Would hate it!) hang about her like a burr?

SIR FRANCIS
No — no. But there's a medium, sir, between
Neglect and persecution.

FRANK
Well, I hope
And think I've hit that medium.

SIR FRANCIS
Reginald,
If you were Mabel's lover, or in hope
To be her lover, could you slight her so?

REGINALD
I can't imagine that condition.

SIR FRANCIS
Then
You youngsters are no more your fathers' sons
Than moles are sons of eagles.

FRANK
Rats of cats,
Say, Father.

SIR FRANCIS
Eh! Was that an epigram?
The point, my boy? Because we worry you?

FRANK
Because we scuttle where you used to spring,
And nibble when you used to bite. At least,
You say so — or they say so.

SIR FRANCIS
Heaven forbid!
Tom Jones and Lovelace were not gods of ours.
But if we meant to win and keep a heart
Worth winning and worth keeping, Frank, we knew
We must not seem to slight it. 'Pique and soothe,'
Young Byron bids you — don't stand off and gape.
There may be better means than his, if you
Love as I trust you love her. There's the bell.

[Exeunt

SCENE II. — In the Garden

FRANK and **MABEL**

FRANK
I may not say what any man may say?

MABEL
To me? And any man, you think, may say
Foolish and heartless things to me? or is it
Only the heir of Heron shaw who claims
A right so undeniable?

FRANK
Is the taunt
Fair to yourself or me? You do not think—

MABEL
You have the right to make mock love to me?
I do not.

FRANK
How have you the right to call
Truth mockery, knowing I love you?

MABEL
How should I
Know it? If you mistake me now for Anne,
You may mistake her presently for me.

FRANK
Anne?

MABEL
If you care for either cousin — much,
It ought, by all I ever heard or read.
To be the one you are always bickering with.

FRANK
She does not like me.

MABEL
She, does not dislike.

FRANK
Her liking would not help nor her dislike
Forbid me to be happy. You perhaps —
I can't guess how you can— may think so: she
Cannot. And if I did—worse luck for me!—
What chance should I have? Can you not have seen
— Not once — not ever — how her face and eyes
Change when she looks at Redgie?

MABEL
What! — Absurd!
You love her, and are mad with jealousy.

FRANK
Mad if I am, my madness is to love
You. But you must have seen it.

MABEL
I am not
Jealous.

FRANK
You need not have an eye to see it.
Her voice might tell you, when she speaks to him.

MABEL
The tone is just like yours or mine. Of course
We all make much — or something— of him now;
Since he came back, I mean.

FRANK

From Waterloo;
I knew it— an interesting young cousin. Well,
He does deserve his luck, I know; he did
Always: and you were always good to him.

MABEL

He always needed somebody, poor boy,
To be so.

FRANK

Ah, if that were all! Because
His guardian, my good father, — good to me
Always — his cousin, in whose grounds we now
Walk and discuss him — and his schoolmasters,
You think, were apt—

MABEL

To ill-use him? No; nor yet
Misunderstand him: that I did not mean.
But she who knew him and loved him best is gone —
His aunt and mine— your mother.

FRANK

Yes: she did
Love him! she must have loved his mother more
Than many sisters love each other.

MABEL

More
Than I love Anne or Anne loves me? I hope
Not. But when death comes in— and leaves behind
A child for pledge and for memorial, love
Must naturally feel more — I want the word;
More of a call upon it — not a claim—
A sort of blind and dumb and sweet appeal
Out of the dark, and out of all the light
That burns no more but broods on all the past —
A glowworm on a grave. And you, I know,
Were never jealous: all the house knew that,
And loved you for it as we did.

FRANK

Ah — as you
Did! I'd have had you love me more than they,
If it had not been too great and sweet a thing
For me to dream of.

MABEL
Do not dream at all.
What good can come of dreaming?

FRANK
Less than none,
If dreaming, doubt, or fear, should take away
The little comfort, such as it is — God knows,
Not much, though precious — that your kind last words
Gave me. Too kind they were, Mabel. I was,
And am, jealous of Redgie; more to-night
Than ever: but I will not be.

MABEL
I am sure
You will not. Why?

FRANK
Because I know — I am sure,
Mabel-more sure than you can be of me
Or I can of myself—he would not grudge
Nor envy me my happiness if you-
Could bring yourself to make me happy.

MABEL
Why
Should he?

FRANK
Ask him.

MABEL
A pretty thing to ask!
But, Frank, it's good, and very good, of you
To say so — if you care for me at all,
And think it possible I could care for him.

FRANK
I think it more than possible: but he
Does not. You'll have to tell him. Don't let Anne
Hear you.

MABEL
I would not let her, certainly,
If I were tempted to propose to you.
Do you think that girls — that women do such things?

FRANK

No: but I do think — think, by heaven! I know —
He will not tell you what a child might see,
That he can love, and does, better than I,
And all his heart is set on you. But Anne
Loves him; you must have seen it.

MABEL

You love her.
And do not know it, and take me for her, seeing
Her features in my face, and thinking she
Loves Redgie: is not this the truth? Be frank,
Or change your name for one that means a lie —
Iscariot or Napoleon.

FRANK

God forbid!
I tell you what I am sure of, as I am sure
I wish I were not.

MABEL

Sure? How can you be?

FRANK

Are you not sure? Be honest. Can you say
You doubt he would have told you — what he won't
And can't — had he been heir of Heronshaw
Or Anyshaw? You might have spared that taunt,
Mabel. But can you say it? You never were
A liar, and never can be. Tell him then
The truth he will not tell you.

MABEL

What if he
Rejects me? This is past a joke.

FRANK

It is.

MABEL

I knew you could not love me. Why make love?

FRANK

I love you; but I see how you love him;
And think you are right. He loves you more than I—
Yes, more than I can- — more than most men could
Love even you. You are no mate for me,
I am no mate for you, the song says. Well,

So be it. God send you happiness with him!
He has done more than give you up — give up
AW chance of you — he would not take the chance
That honour, as he thought, forbade. Do you
Reward him.

MABEL
God reward you, Frank! You see
— It's true — I love him.

FRANK
And he will not speak.
Tell him to-morrow — and come in to-night.

[Exeunt

SCENE I. — Another Part of the Grounds

Enter **SIR ARTHUR CLAVERING** and **REGINALD**.

SIR ARTHUR
I'm glad you love the old place: to have you here —
You and the Dilstons — brings my father's time
Back. I might almost be your father, though;
Yours, or your cousins' — Frank's or Mabel's. Time
Slips on like water.

REGINALD
Very softly, here;
Less like the Kielder than the Deadwater
Till both make up the Tyne.

SIR ARTHUR
It wearies you,
Cousin? Make haste then and grow strong and stout,
And ride away to battle; till you can,
I mean to keep you prisoner and be proud
I have a guest who struck beside the Duke
An English stroke at Waterloo.

REGINALD
Beside,
Arthur? There's no one born can boast of that.
The best we can— the very best of us —

Say for each other, is just, we followed him —
His hand and eye and word and thought — and did
What might be of our duty.

SIR ARTHUR
Well, my boy,
Did he do more? You're just a hothead still —
The very schoolboy that I knew you first —
On fire with admiration and with love
Of some one or of something, always. Now,
Who is it — besides your general? who — or which?
Anne's chestnut shell, or Mabel's golden fire —
Her emerald eyes, or Anne's dark violets — eh?
You have them both (a happy hero you!)
Dancing attendance on your highness. Here
Comes Mabel: have you not a glove to throw?

[Enter **MABEL**.

Dear cousin, make him talk to you: to me
He will not; and I have not time to dance
Attendance on him.

[Exit,

REGINALD
Arthur's jokes are not
Diamonds for brilliance: but he's good.

MABEL
Are you?

REGINALD
You never asked me that of old times.

MABEL
No:
That was superfluous: all the household knew
How good a boy you were.

REGINALD
And you? A girl
There was who loved the saddle as well as I,
And was not slower at breaking bounds.

MABEL
You have not
Forgiven me what you suffered for my sake

So often— much too often.

REGINALD
No, of course.
How should I?

MABEL
You remember our old rides—
Tell me about your ride at Waterloo.

REGINALD
More like a swim against a charging sea
It was, than like a race across the moors
Yonder.

MABEL
But when a breaker got you down —
When you lay hurt it might have been to death —
Will you not tell me what you thought of then?

REGINALD
No.

MABEL
Nothing?

REGINALD
Nothing I can tell you of.

MABEL
Was all a mist and whirlwind — like the shore
Out yonder when the north-east wind is high?
That I can fancy. But when sense came back
You thought of nothing you can tell me of,
Reginald? nothing?

REGINALD
Nothing I can tell
Any one — least of all, women or men,
Frank's wife that is to be, Mabel.

MABEL
And where
Has Frank concealed her from all eyes but yours?
You are too sharp-sighted, Redgie.

REGINALD
Did she not

Ask me just now what if she knew— she must
Have known the answer that I could not make—
It was not right or kind to ask?

MABEL
Not she.

REGINALD
Mabel!

MABEL
She's innocent, at least.

REGINALD
You mean —?

MABEL
I mean she is not here. Nor anywhere
But in the silliest dreamiest brain alive—
The blindest head cheating the trustiest heart
That ever made a man — untrustworthy.
You did not dream or think of any old friend —
Anne, Frank, or me— when you were lying, cut down,
Helpless, that hideous summer night? And now
You will not speak or stir? O, Reginald,
Must I say everything — and more — and you
Nothing?

REGINALD
My love! Mabel! What can I?

MABEL
Say
Just that again.

REGINALD
How can it be?

MABEL
My love,
How could it not be?

REGINALD
How have I deserved
This?

MABEL
How can I tell you? Do you tell me

Now, what you would not tell Frank's wife.

REGINALD
You know
I need not tell you.

MABEL
Tell me, though.

REGINALD
I thought,
Between the shoots and swoonings, off and on,
How hard it was, if anything was hard
When one was dying for England, not to see
Mabel, when I could see the stars. I thought
How sweet it was to know they shone on her
Asleep or waking, here at home. I thought
I could have wished, and should not wish, to send
My whole heart's love back as my life went out,
To find her here and clasp her close and say
What I could never — how much I had loved her.
Then
I thought how base and bad a fool I was
To dream of wishing what would grieve her. Then
I think I fell asleep.

MABEL
And that was all,
Redgie?

REGINALD
And that was all, Mabel.

MABEL
You did —
You did not think, if she had known — if she,
Asleep and dreaming here, had dreamed of it —
What love she would have sent you back for yours—
Yours— how could she be worth it? Did you not
See, as you lay — know, as your pain sank down
And died and left you yet not quite asleep—
How past all words she loved you? Reginald!
You did not?

REGINALD
How should I have dreamed of heaven?
I'm not a saint, Mabel.

MABEL

And what am I
Who ask a man what, being the man he is,
He will not ask me — and am not ashamed?

REGINALD

You are more than ever a man whom heaven loved best
Saw shining out of heaven in dreams — more dear,
More wonderful than angels. How you can
Care for me really and truly — care for me,
It beats my wits to guess.

MABEL

It's very strange,
Of course: what is there in you to be loved?

REGINALD

There's many a true word said in jest. But you!
Why, all the world might fall down at your feet
And you not find a man in all the world
Worth reaching out your hand to raise. And I!
The best luck never finds the best man out.
They say; but no man living could deserve
This.

MABEL

Well, you always were the best to me;
The brightest, bravest, kindest boy you were
That ever let a girl misuse him — make
His loving sense of honour, courage, faith,
Devotion, rods to whip him — literally,
You know — and never by one word or look
Protested. You were born a hero, sir.
Deny it, and tell a louder lie than when
You used to take my faults upon you. How
I loved you then, and always! Now, at last.
You see, you make me tell it: which is not
As kind as might be, or as then you were.

REGINALD

I never was or could be fit for you
To glance on or to tread on. You, whose face
Was always all the light of all the world
To me — the sun of suns, the flower of flowers,
The wonder of all wonders — and your smile
The light that lit the dawn up, and your voice
A charm that might have thrilled and stilled the sea--
You, to put out that heavenly hand of yours

And lift up me to heaven, above all stars
But those God gave you for your eyes on earth
That all might know his angel I

MABEL
There — be still.

[Enter **FRANK** at a distance.

Here comes our bridesman — and our matchmaker.
He told me that he loved me yesterday,
But that you loved me better — more than he.
And, Redgie, that you would not tell me so
Till I had made an offer for your hand
A prophet, was he not?

REGINALD
Did he say that?
I'd like to black his boots.

MABEL
You weren't his fag,
Were you? — Well, Frank, you told me yesterday
Nothing but truth; and this has come of it.

FRANK
Your hand in Redgie's? All goes right, then?

MABEL
All:
I did not give him, I confess, a chance.

REGINALD
Frank, I can't look you in the face — and yet
I hope and think I have not played you false.

FRANK
Well, if you swore you had, Redgie my boy,
I'd not believe you. You play false, indeed!
To look me in the face and tell me that
Would need more brass than nature gave your brows.

REGINALD
But how to look your father in the face —
Upon my honour! You must help me, Frank.

FRANK
And that I will, Redgie. But don't you dream

He'll think there's any need of any help,
Excuse, or pretext for you. Any fool
Must have foreseen it.

MABEL
Yes — I think he must.
Any but one, at least — who would not see.
Frank, I proposed to him — I did. He is
So scandalously stupid!

FRANK
Ah, you know,
I told you. That was unavoidable.

REGINALD
You sons and daughters of good luck and wealth
Make no allowance — cannot, I suppose —
For such poor devils as poor relations. Frank,
I think I see you— in my place, I mean—
Making the least love in the world to her —
Letting her dream you loved her!

FRANK
Well, did you?

MABEL
He did.

REGINALD
I don't know how I did.

MABEL
But I
Know.

FRANK
I can guess. He never dropped a word
Nor looked a look to say it — and so you knew.

MABEL
Yes; that was it.

FRANK
When I go courting, then,
I'll take a leaf out of old Redgie's book,
And never risk a whisper— never be
Decently civil. Well, it's good to see
How happy you two are.

MABEL
Hush! Here comes Anne.

[Enter **ANNE**.

ANNE
I heard what Frank said. And I hope you are
Happy, and always will be.

REGINALD
Thanks. And yet
I know I ought not.

ANNE
Complimentary, that,
To Mabel.

REGINALD
Mabel understands.

ANNE
Of course.
She always understood you.

REGINALD
Did she? No:
She always made too much of me — and now
Much more too much than ever. God knows why.

ANNE
God knows what happiness I wish you both.

REGINALD
Thank her, Mabel.

MABEL
I can't. She frightens me.
Anne!

ANNE
Am I grown frightful to all of you?
Are you afraid of me, Reginald?

REGINALD
What
Can ail you, Mabel? What can frighten you?

ANNE

Excitement — passionate happiness—I see.
Enough to make a girl — before men's eyes —
Shrink almost from her sister.

MABEL

Anne, you knew
This was to be — if Redgie pleased.

ANNE

I did;
And did not doubt it would be.

FRANK

These are strange
Congratulations. Anne, you must have thought
It would not.

ANNE

What I thought or did not think
I know perhaps as well as you. And now
I need not surely twice congratulate
My sister and my brother — soon to be.

MABEL

Let us go in.

ANNE

You seem so happy too
That we must all congratulate you, Frank.

[Exeunt.

ACT III

SCENE I. — In the Garden

ANNE and **MABEL**.

ANNE

This heartsease bed is richer than it was
Last year — and so it should be; should it not?
For your sake and for his, I mean. See here;
Here's one all black — a burning cloud of black,
With golden sunrise at its heart; and here's
One all pure gold from shapely leaf to leaf,

And just its core or centre black as night.

MABEL
They call them pansies too, you know.

ANNE
But you
Must call them heartsease now. Tell me — what thoughts
Have lovers that the lovely plain old name
Would not suit better than all others?

MABEL
None,
None that I know of—nor does Redgie. Anne,
How can we two thank God enough?

ANNE
I'm sure
I cannot tell you, Mabel. All your thoughts
Are flowers, you say, and flowers as sweet as these
Whose perfume makes the rose's coarse and dull
And how then could I tell you how to thank
God? He has given you something— thought or truth.
If truth and thought are not the same— which I
Cannot, you know, imagine,

MABEL
Ah, you will
Some day, and soon — you must and will.

ANNE
I doubt
That. Can the world supply me, do you think,
With such another Redgie?

MABEL
That's not fair.

ANNE
I must put up with something second-rate?
Frank, for example — if he'd have me? No,
Dear Mabel: be content with happiness;
And do not dream it gives you power to play
Providence, or a prophet. Is he not
Waiting for you — there, by the hawthorns — there —
And, certainly, not wanting me?

MABEL

He is!
I told him not to come and wait for me.

[Exit

ANNE
I cannot bear it: and I cannot die.

[Enter **SIR ARTHUR**.

SIR ARTHUR
Our lovers are not here? Ah, no; they want
Seclusion— shade and space between the trees
To chirp and twitter. Well, no wonder.

ANNE
No.

SIR ARTHUR
The handsomest and happiest pair they are
That England or Northumberland could show,
Are they not?

ANNE
Yes; Mabel is beautiful,

SIR ARTHUR
You don't think much of Redgie, then?

ANNE
He looks,
With all that light soft shining curly hair,
Too boyish for his years and trade; but men
Don't live or die by their good looks or bad.

SIR ARTHUR
You don't call soldiership a trade? And then,
His years are not so many — not half mine,
And I'm not quite a greybeard.

ANNE
Let him be
Apollo — Apollino if you like,
Your all but girl-faced godling in the hall.
He did not win her with his face or curls.

SIR ARTHUR
I am proud to know he did not. Are not you?

ANNE
Proud of him? Why should I be?

SIR ARTHUR
No; of her.

ANNE
O! Yes, of course — very. Not every girl,
Of course, would condescend — to look so high.

SIR ARTHUR
A fine young loyal fellow, kind and brave,
Wants no more gilding, does he?

ANNE
Luckily,
We see, he does not. Here she comes alone.
She has sent him in to rest — or speak to Frank.

[Re-enter **MABEL**.

You have not kept him hanging round you long,
You are not exacting, Mabel.

MABEL
Need I be?

ANNE
We see you need not.

SIR ARTHUR
Mabel, may I say
How very and truly glad I am?

MABEL
You may
Indeed, and let me thank you. That you must.

SIR ARTHUR
It makes one laugh, or smile at least, to think
That Master Redgie always was till now
The unlucky boy — the type of luckless youth,
Poor fellow — and now it seems you are going to give
Or rather have given him more than his deserts
Or most men's, if not any man's. I am
Glad.

MABEL
Please don't compliment You know I have known
Reginald all ray life — and can't but know
How much more he deserves than I can give.

ANNE
She has the courage of her faith, you see.

MABEL
Don't play at satire, Annie, when you know
How true it is.

ANNE
Of course I know it, Mab.
He always was incomparable. At school
His masters always said so, and at home—
Ah, well, perhaps the grooms did.

MABEL
One would think
You did not know him, and hated him. I wish
Almost he did not— as he does — deserve
Far more than I shall bring.

SIR ARTHUR
Impossible:
Even if he were — no subaltern, but even
The Duke himself.

[Enter **FRANK** and **REGINALD**.

FRANK
Who's talking of the Duke?
Ask Redgie what he thinks of him.

REGINALD
No, don't.
My name's not Homer.

ANNE
Frenchmen say—

REGINALD
Dear Anne,
Don't you say 'Frenchmen say' — say 'Frenchmen lie.'
They call the man who thrashes them a cur;
Then what must they be?

SIR ARTHUR
Try to tell us, though,
Something — if only to confute the frogs
And shame their craven croaking.

REGINALD
What on earth
Can I or any man — could Wordsworth, even —
Say that all England has not said of him
A thousand times, and will not say again
Ten thousand?

SIR ARTHUR
Come, my boy, you're privileged,
You know: you have served, and seen him.

REGINALD
Seen him? Yes.
You see the sun each morning; but the sun
Takes no particular notice and displays
No special aspect just for your behoof,
Does it?

MABEL
He never spoke to you?

REGINALD
To me?

MABEL
Why not?

REGINALD
He might of course to any one:
But I'm not lucky — never was, you know.

ANNE
They say that none of you who have followed him
Love him as Frenchmen love Napoleon.

REGINALD
No.
How should they? No one loves the sun as much
As drunken fools love wildfires when they go
Plunging through marsh and mire and quag and haugh
To find a filthy grave.

SIR ARTHUR

Come, come, my boy!
Remember — 'love your enemies.'

REGINALD
When I have
Any, I'll try; but not my country's; not
Traitors and liars and thieves and murderers— not
Heroes of French or Irish fashion. Think
How fast the Duke stands always — how there's not
A fellow— can't be— drudging in the rear
Who does not know as well as that the sun
Shines, that the man ahead of all of us
Is fit to lead or send us anywhere
And sure to keep quick time with us, if we
Want or if duty wants him — bids the chief
Keep pace with you or me. And then just think,
Could he, suppose he had been — impossibly —
Beaten and burnt out of the country, lashed,
Lashed like a hound and hunted like a hare
Back to his form or kennel through the snow,
Have left his men dropping like flies, devoured
By winter as if by fire, starved, frozen, blind,
Maimed, mad with torment, dying in hell, while he
Scurried and scuttled off in comfort?

MABEL
No.
He could not. Arthur quite agrees. And now
Be quiet.

SIR ARTHUR
Redgie takes away one's breath.
But that's the trick to catch young ladies' hearts —
Enthusiasm on the now successful side.

MABEL
Successful! If we could have failed, you know,
He would have been — he, I, and you and all,
All of us, all, more passionate and keen
And hotter in our faith and loyalty
And bitterer in our love and hate than now
When thoughts of England and her work are not
Tempered with tears that are not born of pride
And joy that pride makes perfect.

FRANK
Let's be cool.
I have not seen you quite so hot and red

Since you were flogged for bathing at the Weir,
Redgie.

REGINALD
Which time? the twentieth?

FRANK
That at least.

MABEL
Poor fellow!

REGINALD
Ah, you always pitied me —
And spoilt me.

MABEL
No one else did, Reginald.

REGINALD
And right and wise they were— a worthless whelp!

MABEL
Very. Not worth a thought — were you?

REGINALD
I'm sure
Not worth a tear of yours — and yet you cried
Sometimes, you know, for my mischances.

SIR ARTHUR
Ay?
Soj boy and girl were born for bride and groom,
Were they? There's nothing now to cry for, then.

ANNE
Arthur forgets: are love and happiness
Nothing to cry for? Tears, we are told, are signs
Infallible — indispensable — of joy.

FRANK
Mabel and Redgie, then, must be just now
Unhappy — very unhappy. Can they fill
With us their parts to-morrow in his play?

MABEL
Yes: I know mine; and Anne knows hers.

ANNE
And Frank
His. Does he stab you, Redgie, on the stage?

REGINALD
Yes, as I save him from the shipwreck.

SIR ARTHUR
Good!
That's something like a villain.

ANNE
I'm as bad.
I poison Mabel — out of love for Frank.

SIR ARTHUR
Heaven help us, what a tragic day or night!
It's well the drawing-room and the libraries
Are all rigged up ship-shape, with stage and box
Ready, and no such audience to be feared
As might — I don't say would, though, Reginald —
Hiss you from pit and gallery.

REGINALD
That they would!
It's all a theft from Dodsley's great old plays,
I know you'll say — third-rate and second-hand.
The book, you know, you lent me when a boy —
Or else I borrowed and you did not lend.

SIR ARTHUR
That's possible, you bad young scamp, I wish
We could have seen it played in the open air.
Boccaccio-like — but that would scarcely suit
With April in Northumberland.

ANNE
Not quite.

REGINALD
Come, don't abuse our climate and revile
The crowning county of England — yes, the best
It must be.

FRANK
Now he's off again.

REGINALD

I'm not
But I just ask you where you'll find its like?
Have you and I, then, raced across its moors
Till horse and boy were well-nigh mad with glee
So often, summer and winter, home from school,
And not found that out? Take the streams away,
The country would be sweeter than the south
Anywhere: give the south our streams, would it
Be fit to match our borders? Flower an d crag,
Burnside and boulder, heather and whin — you don't
Dream you can match them south of this? And then,
If all the unwatered country were as flat
As the Eton playing-fields, give it back dur burns,
And set them singing through a sad south world,
And try to make them dismal as its fens —
They won't be! Bright and tawny, full of fun
And storm and sunlight, taking change and chance
With laugh on laugh of triumph — why, you know
How they plunge, pause, chafe, chide across the rocks.
And chuckle along the rapids, till they breathe
And rest and pant and build some bright deep bath
For happy boys to dive in, and swim up,
And match the water's laughter.

SIR ARTHUR
You at least
Know it, we doubt not. Woodlands too we have,
Have we not, Mabel? beech, oak, aspen, pine,
And Redgie's old familiar friend, the birch,
With all its blithe lithe bounty of buds and sprays
For hapless boys to wince at, and grow red.
And feel a tingling memory prick their skins—
Sting till their burning blood seems all one blush —
Eh?

REGINALD
I beg pardon if I bored you. But—
You know there's nothing like this country. Frank,
Is there?

FRANK
I never will dispute with you
Anything, Redgie. This is what you call
Being peaceable, is it? firing up like tow
And rattling off like small-shot?

REGINALD
I can't help —

Can I?

FRANK
When you said that at school, my lad.
It didn't help you much.

MABEL
Don't bully him so.
Don't let them, Redgie,

SIR ARTHUR
Redgie must be proof
Now against jokes that used to make the boy
Frown, blush, and wince: and well he may be.

ANNE
Why?
Is Reginald much wiser than he was?
He seems to me the same boy still.

SIR ARTHUR
He is,
I think; but now the luckiest living.

REGINALD
Yes.
I'm half afraid one ought not anyhow
To be so happy. None of you, I know,
Our brothers and our sister, think it right.
You cannot. Nor do L

SIR ARTHUR
A willow-wreath
For Mabel! Redgie turns her off.

MABEL
He might,
If she would let him: but he'll find her grasp
Tenacious as a viper's. Be resigned,
Redgie: I shall not let you go.

REGINALD
I am
Resigned. But if God bade one rise to heaven
At once, and sit above the happiest there,
Resigned one might be—possibly: but still
Would not one shrink for shame's sake? Look at her
And me!

SIR ARTHUR
I never saw a better match.

MABEL
I never had so sweet a compliment
Paid me. I shan't forget it, Arthur.

REGINALD
What
Possesses ah of you to try and turn
The poor amount of head I have, I can't
Imagine. One might think you had laid a bet
To make a man shed tears by way of thanks
And laugh at him for crying. Frank, — Arthur, — Anne,
You know I know how good it is of you
To wish me joy — and how I thank you: that
You must know.

ANNE
Surely, Reginald, we do.
Goodwill like ours could hardly miss, I trust.
Of gratitude like yours.

MABEL
What is it, Anne?
What makes you smile so?

ANNE
Would you have me frown?

MABEL
Rather than smile like that: you would not look
So enigmatic.

ANNE
Let it pass, my dear;
I've shall not smile to-morrow, when we play
Tragedy— shall we? Are the properties
Ready — stiletto and poison-flask?

REGINALD
Ah, there
We are lucky. There's the old laboratory, made
It seems for our stage purpose, where you know
Sir Edward kept his chemicals and things —
Collections of the uncanniest odds and ends.
Poisons and weapons from all parts of the earth.

Which Arthur lets us choose from.

ANNE
Are they safe
To play with?

MABEL
Are we children, Annie? Still
Perhaps you are right: we had better let them be.

SIR ARTHUR
The daggers are not dangerous — blunt as lead —
That I shall let you youngsters play with.

REGINALD.
Good:
But how about the poison? let us have
A genuine old Venetian flask to fill
With wine and water.

ANNE
Let me choose it.

MABEL
You?
Why?

ANNE
I know more about such things.

MABEL
About
Poison?

ANNE
About the loveliest old-world ware
Fonthill or Strawberry Hill could furnish: I'm
Miss Beckford, or Horatia Walpole.

SIR ARTHUR
Come
And take your choice of the empty flasks. Don't choose
A full one by mistake.

ANNE
I promise not.

[Exeunt **SIR ARTHUR** and **ANNIE**.

FRANK

I leave you to consult together, then —
The playwright and his heroine: that's but fair.

[Exit.

MABEL

I don't quite like it, Redgie: I'm afraid
Anne is not happy: I'm afraid.

REGINALD

My love;
Is any one unhappy in the world?
I can't just now believe in wretchedness.

MABEL

But I can. Redgie, do be good — and grave.
I talk to you as if you were grown-up,
You see.

REGINALD

You do me too much honour.

MABEL

That
I do, you stupidest of tiresome boys.
Still, you were never ill-natured, were you? Well,
Have you not — boys see nothing — don't you think
You might have seen, had you but eyes, that Anne
Is not— I don't say (that would be absurd)
As happy as we are — no one could be that —
But not— not happy at all?

REGINALD

My darling, no.
What dream is this — what lunacy of love?

MABEL

Well — I must tell you everything, I see—
I wish I did not and I could not think
Her heart or fancy— call it either— were
More fixed on Frank than ever his on me.

REGINALD

Eh! Well, why not? If he can come to love
Any one, after thinking once he loved
You — and you would not have it break his heart

Quite, would you?— what could well befall us all
Happier than this? You don't suppose he can?
To me it seems — you know how hard and strange
It seems to hope or fancy: but God grant
It may be! If old Frank were happy once,
I should not feel I ought not — now and then —
To be so happy always.

MABEL
But you ought.
How good you are, Redgie!

REGINALD
O, very good.
I'd like — I want — to see my dearest friends
Happy— without a touch of trouble or pains
For me to take or suffer. Wonderful,
Is it not? saintly — great — heroic?

MABEL
Well,
I think you may— I think we shall. But don't
Be boyish— don't be prompting Frank; you know,
Reginald, what I mean.

REGINALD
Yes: that he may —
Will, very likely — want a hand like yours
Rather than mine to help him — bring him through —
Give him a lift or shove.

MABEL
Leave well alone.
That's all I mean.

REGINALD
You always did know best,
And always will: I shall be always right
Now that my going or doing or saying depends
On you. It's well you are what you are: you might,
If you were evil-minded, make a man
Run from his post — betray or yield his flag —
Duck down his head and scuttle.

MABEL
Not a man
Like you.

REGINALD
Let no man boast himself; does not
The Bible say — something like that?

MABEL
Perhaps.
But then you don't, and never did, you know —
Not even about this play of yours. Come in:
The windy darkness creeps and leaps by fits
Up westward: clouds, and neither stars nor sun,
And just the ghost of a lost moon gone blind
And helpless. If we are to play at all,
I must rehearse my part again to-night.

[Exeunt.

ACT IV

SCENE I. — A Stage Representing a Garden by the Sea

SONG (from within).
Love and Sorrow met in May
Crowned with rue and hawthorn-spray,
    And Sorrow smiled.
Scarce a bird of all the spring
Durst between them pass and sing,
    And scarce a child.
Love put forth his hand to take
Sorrow's wreath for sorrow's sake,
    Her crown of rue.
Sorrow cast before her down
Even for love's sake Love's own crown,
    Crowned with dew.
Winter breathed again, and spring
Cowered and shrank with wounded wing
    Down out of sight.
May, with all her loves laid low,
Saw no flowers but flowers of snow
    That mocked her flight.
Love rose up with crownless head
Smiling' down on springtime dead,
    On wintry May.
Sorrow, like a cloud that dies,
Like a cloud in clearing skies,
    Passed away.

[Enter **ALVISE**.

ALVISE
This way she went: the nightingales that heard
Fell silent, and the loud-mouthed salt sea-wind
Took honey on his lips from hers, and breathed
The new-born breath of roses. Not a weed
That shivers on the storm-shaped lines of shore
But felt a fragrance in it, and put on
The likeness of a lily.

[Enter **GALASSO**.

GALASSO
Thou art here.
God will not let thee hide thyself too close
For hate and him to find thee. Draw: the light
Is good enough to die by.

ALVISE
Thou hast found him
That would have first found thee. Set thou thy sword
To mine, its edge is not so fain to bite
As is my soul to slay thee.

[They draw.

[Enter **BEATRICE** and **FRANCESCA**

BEATRICE
What is this?
What serpent have ye trod on?

ALVISE
Didst thou bid me
Draw, seeing far off the surety for thy life
That women's tongues should bring thee?

BEATRICE
Speak not to him.
Speak to me— me, Alvise.

ALVISE
Sweet, be still.
Galasso, shall I smite thee on the lips
That dare not answer with a lie to mine
And know they cannot, if they speak, but lie?

GALASSO
Thou knowest I dare not in Beatrice's sight
Strike thee to hell — nor threaten thee.

ALVISE
I know
Thou liest. She stands between thy grave and thee,
As thou between the sun and hell.

FRANCESCA
My lord,
Forbear him.

GALASSO
I am not thy lord; who made me
Master or lord of thine? Not God should say,
Save with his tongue of thunder, and be heard
(If hearing die not in a dead man's ear),
'Forbear him.'

ALVISE
Nay, Beatrice, bid not me
Forbear: he will not let me bid him live.

GALASSO
Thou shalt not find a tongue some half-hour hence
To pray with to my sword for time to pray
And die not damned.

FRANCESCA
Sir, speak not blasphemy.
Death's wings beat round about us day and night:
Their wind is in our faces now. I pray you,
Take heed.

GALASSO
Of what? of God, or thee? Not I.
But let Beatrice bend to me —

ALVISE
To thee?
Bend? Nay, Beatrice, bind me not in chains,
Who would not play thy traitor: give my sword
What God gives all the waves and birds of the air,
Freedom.

BEATRICE
He gives it not to slay.

ALVISE
He shall.
Are the waves bloodless or the vultures bland?
Loose me, love: leave me: let me go.

BEATRICE
Thou shalt not
Put off for me before my face thy nature,
Thy natural name of man, to mock with murder
The murderous waves and beasts of ravin. Slay me.
And God may give thee leave to slay him: I
Shall know not of it ever.

GALASSO
Vivarini,
These women's hands that here strike peace between us
To-morrow shall not stead thee. Live a little:
My sword is not more thirsty than the sea,
Nor less secure in patience. Thou shalt find
A sea-rock for thy shipwreck on dry land here
When thou shalt steer again upon the steel of it
And find its fang's edge mortal.

[Exit.

ALVISE
Have ye shamed me?
Mine enemy goes down seaward with no sign
Set of my sword upon him.

BEATRICE
Let him pass.
To-morrow brings him back from sea— if ever
He come again.

FRANCESCA
How should not he come back, then?

BEATRICE
The sea hath shoals and storms.

ALVISE
God guard him — till
He stand within my sword's reach!

FRANCESCA
Pray thou rather

God. keep thee from the reach of his.

ALVISE
He cannot,
Except he smite to death or deadly sickness
One of us ere we join. My saint Beatrice,
Thou hast no commission, angel though thou be, sweet,
Given thee of God to guard mine enemy's head
Or cross me as his guardian.

BEATRICE
Would I cross thee,
The spirit I live by should stand up to chide
The soul-sick will that moved me. Yet I would not,
Had I God's leave in hand to give thee, give
Thy sword and his such leave to cross as might
Pierce through my heart in answer.

ALVISE
Wouldst thou bid me,
When he comes back to-morrow from the sea
Whereon to-day his ship rides royal, yield
Thee and my sword up to him?

FRANCESCA
Nay, not her:
Thy sword she might.

ALVISE
She would not.

BEATRICE
Fain I would,
And keep thine honour perfect.

ALVISE
That may be,
When heaven and hell kiss, and the noon puts on
The starry shadow of midnight. Sweet, come in;
The wind grows keener than a flower should face
And fear no touch of trouble. Doubt me not
That I will take all heed for thee and me,
Who am now no less than one least part of thee.

[Exeunt.

SCENE II. — The Same

Enter **BEATRICE** and **FRANCESCA**.

BEATRICE
The wind is sharp as steel, and all the sky
That is not red as molten iron black
As iron long since molten. How the flowers
Cringe down and shudder from the scourge! I would
Galasso's ship were home in harbour,

FRANCESCA
Here?
What comfort wouldst thou give him?

BEATRICE
What should I give?
Hadst thou some gentler maiden's mercy in thee,
Thou might'st, though death hung shuddering on his lips
And mixed its froth of anguish with the sea's,
Revive him.

FRANCESCA
I, Beatrice?

BEATRICE
Who but thou,
Francesca?

FRANCESCA
Mock not, lest thy scoff turn back
Like some scared snake to sting thee.

BEATRICE
Nay, not I:
Dost thou not mock me rather, knowing I know
Thou lov'st him as I love not? as I love
Alvise?

FRANCESCA
There is none I love but God.
Thou knowest he doth not love me.

BEATRICE
Dost thou dream
His love for me is even as thine for him,
Born of a braver father than is hate,
A fairer mother than is envy? Me

He loves not as he hates my lover; thou
Mayst haply set — as in this garden-ground
Half barren and all bitter from the sea
Some light of lilies shoots the sun's laugh back—
Even in the darkness of his heart and hate
Some happier flower to spring against thy smile
And comfort thee with blossom,

FRANCESCA
Thou shouldst be not
So fast a friend of mine: we were not born
I a Mariani, a Signorelli thou,
To play, with love and hate at odds with life,
Sisters.

BEATRICE
I know not in what coign of the heart
The root of hate strikes hellward, nor what rains
Make fat so foul a spiritual soil with life,
Nor what plague-scattering planets feed with fire
Such earth as brings forth poison. What is hate
That thou and I should know it?

FRANCESCA
I cannot tell.
Flowers are there deadlier than all blights of the air
Or hell's own reek to heavenward: springs, whose water
Puts out the pure and very fire of life
As clouds may kill the sunset: sins and sorrows,
Hate winged as love, and love walled round as hate is,
With fear and weaponed wrath and arm-girt anguish,
There have been and there may be. Wouldst thou dream now
This flower were mortal poison, or this flasket
Filled full with juice of colder-blooded flowers
And herbs the faint moon feeds with dew, that warily
I bear about me against the noonday's needs,
When the sun ravins and the waters reek
With lustrous fume and feverous light like fire,
Preservative against it?

BEATRICE
Sure, the flower
Could hurt no babe as bright and soft as it
More than it hurts us now to smell to: nor
Could any draught that heals or harms be found
Preservative against it.

FRANCESCA

Yet perchance
Preservative this draught of mine might prove
Against the bitterness of life— of noon,
I would say — heat, and heavy thirst, and faintness
That binds with lead the lids of the eyes, and hangs
About the heart like hunger.

BEATRICE
I am athirst;
Thy very words have made me: and the noon
Indeed is hot Let me drink of it.

FRANCESCA
Drink.

BEATRICE
The wells are not so heavenly cold. What comfort
Thou hast given me! I shall never thirst again,
I think.

FRANCESCA
I am sure thou shalt not— till thou wake
Out of the next kind sleep that shall fall on thee
And hold thee fast as love, an hour or twain hence.

BEATRICE
I thank thee for thy gentle words and promises
More than for this thy draught of healing. Sleep
Is half the seed of life — the seed and stay of it —
And love is all the rest.

FRANCESCA
Thou art sure of that?
Be sure, then.

BEATRICE
How should I be less than sure of it?
Alvise's love and thine confirm and comfort
Mine own with like assurance. All the wind's wrath
That darkens now the whitening sea to southward
Shall never blow the flame that feeds the sun out
Nor bind the stars from rising: how should grief, then,
Evil, or envy, change or chance of ruin,
Lay hand on love to mar him? Death, whose tread
Is white as winter's ever on the sea
Whose waters build his charnel, hath no kingdom
Beyond the apparent verge and bourn of life
Whereon to reign or threaten. Love, not he,

Is lord of chance and change: the moons and suns
That measure time and lighten serve him not,
Nor know they if a shadow at all there be
That fear and fools call death, not seeing each year
How thick men's dusty days and crumbling hours
Fall but to rise like stars and bloom like flowers.

[Exeunt.

SCENE III. — The Same

Enter **ALVISE** and **BEATRICE**.

ALVISE
Thou art not well at ease: come in again
And rest: the day grows dark as nightfall, ere
Night fall indeed upon it.

BEATRICE
No, not yet,
I do not fear the thunder, nor the sea
That mocks and mates the thunder. What I fear
I know not: but I will not go from hence
Till that sea-thwarted ship's crew thwart the sea
Or perish for its pasture. See, she veers,
And sets again straight hither. All good saints,
Whose eyes unseen of ours that here lack light
Hallow the darkness, guard and guide her! Lo,
She reels again, and plunges shoreward: God,
Whose hand with curb immeasurable as they
Bridles and binds the waters, bid the wind
Fall down before thee silent ere it slay,
And death, whose clarion rends the heart of the air,
Be dumb as now thy mercy! O, that cry
Had more than tempest in it; life borne down
And hope struck dead with horror there put forth
Toward heaven that heard not for the clamouring sea
Their last of lamentation.

ALVISE
Some there are —
Nay, one there is comes shoreward. If mine eyes
Lie not, being baffled of the wind and sea,
The face that flashed upon us out of hell
Between the refluent and the swallowing wave
Was none if not Galasso's. Nay, go in;

Look not upon us.

BEATRICE
Wherefore?

ALVISE
Must I not
Save him to slay to-morrow? If I let
The sea's or God's hand slay mine enemy first,
That hand strikes dead mine honour.

[Exit

BEATRICE
Save him, Christ!
God, save him! Death is at my heart: I feel
His breath make darkness round me.

[Enter **FRANCESCA**.

FRANCESCA
Dost thou live?
Dost thou live yet?

BEATRICE
I know not. What art thou,
To question me of life and death?

FRANCESCA
I am not
The thing I was.

BEATRICE
The friend I loved and knew thee,
Thou art not. This fierce night that leaps up eastward.
Laughing with hate and hunger, loud and blind,
Is not less like the sunrise. What strange poison;
Has changed thy blood, that face and voice and spirit
(If spirit or sense bid voice or face interpret)
Should change to this that meets me?

FRANCESCA
Did I drink
The poison that I gave thee? Thou art dead now:
Not the oldest of the world's forgotten dead
Hath less to do than thou with life. Thou shalt not
Set eyes again on one that loved thee: here
No face but death's and mine, who hate thee deadlier

Than life hates death, shalt thou set eyes on. Die,
And dream that God may save thee; from my hands
Alive thou seest he could not.

[Re-enter **ALVISE** with **GALASSO**.

ALVISE
Stand, I say.
Stand up. Thou hast no hurt upon thee. Stand,
And gather breath to praise God's grace with.

GALASSO
Thee
First must I thank, who hast plucked me hardly back
Forth of the ravening lips of death. What art thou?
This light is made of darkness.

ALVISE
Yet the darkness
May serve to see thine enemy by: to-morrow
The sun shall serve us better when we meet
And sword to sword gives thanks for sword-strokes.

GALASSO
No:
The sun shall never see mine enemy more
Now that his hand has humbled me.

ALVISE
Forego not
Thy natural right of manhood. Chance it was.
Not I, that chose thee for my hand to save
As haply thine had saved me, had the wind
Flung me as thee to deathward.

GALASSO
Dost thou think
To live, and say it, and smile at me? Thy saint
Had heavenlier work to do than guard thee, when
God gave thine evil star such power as gave thee
Power on thine enemy's life to save it. Twice
Thou shalt not save or spare me: if to-morrow
Thy sword had borne down mine, thou hadst let me live
And shamed me out of living: now, I am sure,
Thou shalt not twice rebuke me.

[Stabs Him.

BEATRICE
Death is good:
He gives me back Alvise.

ALVISE
Was it thou
Or God, Beatrice, speaking out of heaven,
Who turned my death to life?

BEATRICE
I am dying, Alvise:
I thought to have left — perchance to have lost thee: now
We shall not part for ever.

[Dies. **ALVISE** dies.

FRANCESCA
Wilt thou stand
Star-struck to death, Galasso? Let our dead
Lie dead, while we fly fleet as birds or winds
Forth of the shadow of death, and laugh, and live
As happy as these were hapless.

GALASSO
She — is she
Dead? Hath she kissed the death upon his lips
And fed it full from hers?

FRANCESCA
Why, dost thou dream
I did not kill her?

GALASSO
Not a devil in hell
But one cast forth on earth could do it: and she
Shall shame the light of heaven no longer.

[Stabs her.

FRANCESCA
Fool,
Thou hast set me free from fate and fear: I knew
Thou wouldst not love me.

[Dies.

GALASSO
What am I, to live

And see this death about me? Death and life
Cast out so vile a thing from sight of heaven.
Save, where the darkness of the grave is deep,
I cannot think to wake on earth or sleep.

SCENE I.—An Ante-Chamber to the Drawing-Room

Enter **ANNE**.

ANNE
To bear my death about me till I die
And always put the time off, tremblingly.
As if I loved to live thus, would be worse
Than death and meaner than the sin to die.
The sin to kill myself— or think of it —
I have sinned that sin already. Not a day
That brings the day I cannot live to see
Nearer, but burns my heart like flame and makes
My thoughts within me serpents fanged with fire.
He would not weep if I were dead, and she
Would. If I make no better haste to die,
I shall go mad and tell him— pray to him,
If not for love, for mercy on me — cry
'Look at me once'— not as you look at her,
But not as every day you look at me —
And see who loves you, Reginald.' Ah God,
That one should yearn at heart to do or say
What if it ever could be said or done
Would strike one dead with shame!

MABEL (singing in the next room)
There's nae lark loves the lift, my dear,
There's nae ship loves the sea,
There's nae bee loves the heather-bells,
That loves as I love thee, my love,
That loves as I love thee.

The whin shines fair upon the fell,
The blithe broom on the lea;
The muirside wind is merry at heart:
It's a' for love of thee, my love,
It's a' for love of thee.

ANNE

For love of death,
For love of death it is that all things live
And all joys bring forth sorrows. Sorrow and death
Have need of life and love to prey upon
Lest they too die as these do. What am I
That I should live? A thousand times it seems
I have drawn this flasket out to look on it
And dream of dying, since first I seized it— stole,
And Arthur never missed it. Yet again
The thought strikes back and stabs me, what are they.
What are they all, that they should live, and I
Die? Arthur told me, surely, that this death
Was pangless — swift and soft as when betimes
We sink away to sleep. If sin it is,
I will die praying for pardon: God must see
I am no more fit to live than is a bird
Wounded to death.

[Enter **SIR FRANCIS**, **SIR ARTHUR**, and **FRANK**.

SIR FRANCIS
Well, Anne, and could you rest
Well after murdering Mabel? Here is Frank
Declares his crimes would hardly let him sleep;
While he who made you criminals appears
Shamelessly happy.

FRANK
Redgie always was
Hardened: the plays he used to improvise
At school were deep in bloodshed.

SIR ARTHUR
Let us trust
That happiness and age may make his Muse
Milder.

ANNE
I am sure I hope so. It was hard
To find yourself so wicked.

SIR FRANCIS
Hard on you,
Certainly. Were you tired?

ANNE
Why? Do I look
Tired?

SIR FRANCIS
Well, not tired exactly; still, your eyes
Look hot and dull.

ANNE
All eyes cannot be bright
Always, like Reginald's and Mabel's.

SIR ARTHUR
Ah,
It does one good to see them. Since the world
Began, or love began it, never was
A brighter pair of lovers. What a life
Will theirs be, if the morning of it mean
Really the thing it seems to say, and noon
Keep half the promise of it!

FRANK
That it should,
If they get only their deserts; they are,
He the best fellow, she the best girl born.

SIR FRANCIS
You're not a bad friend, Frank, I will say.

ANNE
No.
He is not.

SIR FRANCIS
What your father would have said
To my approval of the match, perhaps
It's best not guessing: but the harshest brute
That ever made his broken-hearted ward
The subject or the heroine of a tale
Must, I think, have relented here.

SIR ARTHUR
But Still
We are none the less your debtors— Redgie and I.
It lays on me an obligation too.
Your generous goodness to him.

SIR FRANCIS
No, none at all.
I would not let the youngster tell me so.

[Enter **REGINALD** and **MABEL**.

So, you can look us in the face, my boy,
And not be, as you should, ashamed to see
How much less happy are other folk than you?
Your face is like the morning.

REGINALD
Does it blush?
You'd see I was ashamed then. '

MABEL
What, of me,
Redgie? Ifs rather soon to say so. Still,
It's not too late — happily.

SIR FRANCIS
Nothing can
Happen that does not fall out happily,
It seems, for you— and nothing should, I think,
Ever. Come with me, Frank: I want you.

FRANK
Why?

SIR FRANCIS
I never thought you quite so dull till now.
Come.

[Exeunt **SIR FRANCIS** and **FRANK**.

SIR ARTHUR
Take me with you: I'm superfluous too.

[Exit,

MABEL
Don't you go, Anne.

ANNE
I will not if you wish.

MABEL
I do, and so does Redgie. We have seen
These last few days as little of you, you know,
As if you had been — well, anywhere.

ANNE

Except,
Remember, at rehearsals? and last night
We came against each other on the stage.

MABEL
Indeed we did. Is that a property
You have kept about you?

ANNE
What? where? this — ah no,
A— something for a touch of cold I caught
Last night — I think at least it was last night.
Arthur prescribed it for me.

MABEL
Let me taste.
I am hoarse — I am sure I must be hoarse to-day
With rattling out all Redgie's rant— much more
Than you did.

ANNE
No; you do not want it

MABEL
Anne!

ANNE
You cannot want it, Mabel.

MABEL
How can you
Know? Don't be positive — and selfish.

ANNE
There —
Take it. No — do not taste it, Mabel.

MABEL
Look,
Redgie, how strange a pretty colour! Why,
One wants a name to praise it — and it smells
Like miles on miles of almond-blossom, all
Condensed in one full flower. If this had been
The poison Anne and you prepared for me,
I really would have taken it last night
And not pretended, as I did, to sip,
And kept my lips dry.

[Drinks.

REGINALD
Does the flavour match
The colour?

MABEL
It's a sweet strange taste. Don't you
Try: you won't like it.

REGINALD
Let me know, at least,

[Drinks.

ANNE
You do not yet: or do you now know?

MABEL
Anne!
What have we done and you? What is it?

ANNE
Death,
Mabel. You see, you would not let me die
And leave you living.

MABEL
Death? She is mad — she is mad!
Reginald, help us — her and me — but her
First.

REGINALD
I can hardly help myself to stand.
Sit you down by me.

ANNE
Can the sun still shine?
I did not mean to murder you.

MABEL
And yet
We are dying, are we not— dying?

ANNE
I meant
To die, and never sin again or see
How happy past all dreams of happiness

You, whom he loved, and he, who loved you, were.

[Re-enter **SIR FRANCIS**, **SIR ARTHUR**, and **FRANK**.

SIR FRANCIS
We are here again, you see, already. Why,
What strange new tragic play is this you are all
Rehearsing?

ANNE
Mabel, if you can forgive,
Say so. I may remember that in hell.

MABEL
I do. And so does Redgie, But you might
Have spared or saved him.

ANNE
How, and let you die?

REGINALD
Ah, how? She did not mean it.

ANNE
And do you
Forgive me?

REGINALD
Surely, I am one with her,
And she forgives.

SIR ARTHUR
They are dying indeed. And she
Has killed them.

REGINALD
No. She did not mean.

MABEL
Indeed,
She did not.

SIR FRANCIS
Godin heaven! What dream is this?

ANNE
God help me! But God will not. I must die
Alone, if they forgive me. I must die.

[Exit.

REGINALD
It was a terrible accident, you see—
Was it not, Mabel? That is all we know.

MABEL
All.

FRANK
Redgie, will you speak to me?

REGINALD
Good night,
Frank — dear old Frank — my brother and hers. And you,
Good night, dear Arthur. Think we are going to see
Our mother, Mabel — Frank's and ours.

MABEL
I will.
But, Reginald, how hard it is to go!

REGINALD
We have been so happy, darling, let us die
Thinking of that, and thanking, God.

MABEL
I will.
Kiss me. Ah, Redgie!

[Dies.

REGINALD
Mabel! I am here.

[Dies.

SIR ARTHUR
They could have lived no happier than they die.

Algernon Charles Swinburne – A Short Biography

Algernon Charles Swinburne was born at 7 Chester Street, Grosvenor Place, in London, on April 5th, 1837. He was the eldest of six children born to Captain Charles Henry Swinburne and Lady Jane Henrietta, daughter of the 3rd Earl of Ashburnham, a wealthy Northumbrian family.

Swinburne spent his early years at East Dene in Bonchurch, on the Isle of Wight. As a child, Swinburne was nervous and frail, but also imbued with a nervous energy and fearlessness almost to the point of recklessness.

He was schooled at Eton College from 1849 to 1853. It was here that he first began to write poetry. He excelled at languages and whilst still at Eton won first prizes in both French and Italian.

From Eton he moved to Oxford where he attended at Balliol College from 1856. Here he met friends to whom he became closely attached, among them Dante Gabriel Rossetti, William Morris and Edward Burne-Jones, who in 1857, were painting their Arthurian murals on the walls of the Oxford Union. At Oxford Swinburne was mentored by Benjamin Jowett, the master of Balliol College, who recognised his poetic talent and, intervening on his behalf, tried to keep him from being expelled when he celebrated the Italian patriot Orsini, and his failed attempt on the life of Napoleon III in 1858. Swinburne had to leave the Universcity for a few months due to this but returned in May, 1860 but never received a degree.

Summers were usually spent at Capheaton Hall in Northumberland, the house of his grandfather, Sir John Swinburne, 6th Baronet, who had a famous library and was himself President of the Literary and Philosophical Society in Newcastle upon Tyne.

Swinburne proudly considered himself a native of Northumberland and this is reflected in poems such as the intensely patriotic 'Northumberland' and 'Grace Darling'. He enjoyed riding across the moors and was, it was said, a daring horseman, as he moved 'through honeyed leagues of the northland border', as he remembered the Scottish border in his Recollections.

In the period from 1857 to 1860, Swinburne was one of a number of Pre-Raphaelite's who visited and became part of Lady Pauline Trevelyan's intellectual circle at Wallington Hall, a few miles west of Morpeth in Northumberland.

After leaving college, he moved to London and began his career in earnest as well as becoming a constant visitor to the Rossetti's house. To Rossetti Swinburne was his 'little Northumbrian friend', an affectionate reference to Swinburne's small stature—a mere five foot four. Whatever Swinburne lacked in height he made up for in poetic talent. However, with the burden of such great talent came the unveiling of a dark side that was to cause him pain and would, at times, threaten his very existence with all manner of self-inflicted pains through drink, drugs and sado-machoism.

In 1860 Swinburne published two verse dramas; The Queen Mother and Rosamond but it would not be until 1865 that Swinburne would achieve literary success with Atalanta in Calydon.

In 1861, Swinburne visited Menton on the French Riviera to recover from the effects of yet another period of excess use of alcohol, staying at the Villa Laurenti. From Menton, Swinburne then travelled on to Italy, where he journeyed widely.

After Elizabeth Rossetti's death from suicide in 1862, he and Rossetti moved to Tudor House at 16 Cheyne Walk in Chelsea. The stories that survive from his year with Rossetti are typical Swinburne. In one, Rossetti once had to tell him to keep down the noise — he and a boyfriend had been sliding naked down the bannisters and disturbing Rossetti's painting. He took a sardonic delight in what the critic and biographer, Cecil Lang, calls "Algernonic exaggeration": When people began to talk scathingly about his homosexuality and other sexual proclivities, he circulated a story that he had engaged in pederasty and bestiality with a monkey — and then eaten it. How many of the stories were true and how many invented is unclear. Oscar Wilde called him "a braggart in matters of vice, who had done everything he could to convince his fellow citizens of his homosexuality and bestiality without being in the slightest degree a homosexual or a bestialiser."

In December 1862, Swinburne accompanied Scott and his guests on a trip to Tynemouth. Scott writes in his memoirs that, as they walked by the sea, Swinburne declaimed the as yet unpublished 'Hymn to Proserpine' and 'Laus Veneris' in his lilting intonation, while the waves 'were running the whole length of the long level sands towards Cullercoats and sounding like far-off acclamations'.

Swinburne possessed a curious combination of frail health and strength. He was small and slightly built, but an excellent swimmer and the first to climb Culver Cliff on the Isle of Wight. He had an extremely excitable disposition: people who met him described him as a "demoniac boy" who would go skipping about the room declaiming poetry at the top of his voice. In this as in many things, moderation was not the standard for him. Excess was. Once or twice he had fits, thought to be epileptic, in public; but he made this condition much worse by drinking past excess to unconsciousness. More than once he was delivered to the door in the small of the night, dead drunk. Throughout the 1860s and '70s he rode an alcoholic cycle of dissolution, collapse, drying out at home in the country, then returning to London where he would begin the cycle all over again.

His mania for masochism, particularly flagellation, most probably started in early childhood at Eton and was encouraged by his later friendships with Richard Monckton Milnes (one of Tennyson's fellow Apostles), who introduced him to the works of the Marquis de Sade, and Richard Burton, the Victorian explorer and adventurer. Swinburne was an alcoholic and algolagniac (a desire for sexual gratification through inflicting pain on oneself or others; sadomasochism). He found life difficult, unfulfilling but still his poetic talents pushed to the fore.

Although Swinburne continued to publish some works in periodicals in 1865 he was granted recognition by both public and critics with Atalanta in Calydon written in the style of a classical Greek tragedy.

There followed "Laus Veneris" and Poems and Ballads (1866), with their sexually charged passages, absolutely decadent for polite Victorian society, which were attacked all the more violently as a result. The poems written in homage of Sappho of Lesbos such as "Anactoria" and "Sapphics" were especially savaged. The volume also contained poems such as "The Leper," "Laus Veneris," and "St Dorothy" which evoke both Swinburne's and a general Victorian fascination with the Middle Ages, and are explicitly mediaeval in style, tone and construction. With its publication came instant notoriety. He was now identified with indecent and decadent themes and the precept of art for art's sake.

Swinburne's meeting in 1867 with his long-time hero Mazzini, the Italian patriot living in England in exile, was the beginning of a poetical journey that now became more serious and more engaged with serious thought, initially leading to the political poems in the volume Songs Before Sunrise.

Also in 1867 he was introduced to Adah Isaacs Menken, the American actress, poet and circus rider, whose main fame seemed to be riding naked on a horse (in fact she wore tight nude coloured clothing) for her performance in the melodrama Mazeppa (itself based on a poem by Lord Byron). Although they had a short affair Adah's quote implies that Swinburne was not ready for a relationship that did not involve some self-sabotage; "I can't make him understand that biting's no use."

In 1879, with Swinburne nearly dead from alcoholism and dissolution, his legal advisor Theodore Watts-Dunton took him in, and was gradually successful in getting him to adapt to a healthier lifestyle. Swinburne lived the rest of his life at Watts-Dunton's house. He saw less and less of his old bohemian friends, who thought him a prisoner at The Pines, but his growing deafness also accounts for some of his decreased sociability. By now Swinburne was 42, and was moving from a young man of rebelliousness to a figure of social respectability. It was said of Watts-Dunton that he saved the man and killed the poet.

It is clear that Swinburne had an addictive personality, and clearly incapable of moderation in his pursuit of any chosen vices. This, of course, would both nourish and perhaps sabotage his poetic career. His poetry follows the somewhat clichéd pattern of early flourish and later decline; indeed some of the fresher pieces in the second and third series of Poems and Ballads (published in 1878 and 1889) were actually written during his days at Oxford. Nevertheless, his last collection, A Channel Passage, has some beautiful poems, including "The Lake of Gaube."

He is best remembered as the supreme technician in metre, with a versatility which exceeds even Tennyson's, but which lacks a corresponding emotional range. His obsessions are not widely enough shared; and if he cannot shock us by the strangeness of his desires nor the shrillness of his anti-theistical exclamations, often what remains is not enough to fully engage with the audience.

Swinburne is considered a poet of the decadent school, although he perhaps professed to more vice than he actually indulged in to advertise his deviance. Common gossip of the time reported that he also had a deep crush on the explorer Sir Richard Francis Burton, despite the fact that Swinburne himself abhorred travel. Fact and fiction are easily absorbed by the other so are difficult to untangle even now.

Many critics consider his mastery of vocabulary, rhyme and metre impressive, although he has also been criticised for his florid style and word choices that only fit the rhyme scheme rather than contributing to the meaning of the piece. A. E. Housman, although a critic, had great praise for his rhyming ability: to Swinburne the sonnet was child's play: the task of providing four rhymes was not hard enough, and he wrote long poems in which each stanza required eight or ten rhymes, and wrote them so that he never seemed to be saying anything for the rhyme's sake.

Throughout his career Swinburne published literary criticism of great worth. His deep knowledge of world literatures contributed to a critical style rich in quotation, allusion, and comparison. He is particularly noted for discerning studies of Elizabethan dramatists and of many English and French poets and novelists. As well he was a noted essayist and wrote two novels.

Swinburne was nominated for the Nobel Prize in Literature every year from 1903 to 1907 and then again in 1909.

H.P. Lovecraft, the master of the dark side and a decent poet himself, considered Swinburne "the only real poet in either England or America after the death of Mr. Edgar Allan Poe."

Swinburne was also responsible for devising a poetic form called the roundel, a variation of the French Rondeau form. In 1883 he published A Century of Roundels with several of the roundels dedicated to Dante's sister, the poet Christina Georgina Rossetti. Swinburne wrote to Edward Burne-Jones in 1883: "I have got a tiny new book of songs or songlets, in one form and all manner of metres ... just coming out, of which Miss Rossetti has accepted the dedication. I hope you and Georgie [his wife Georgiana] will find something to like among a hundred poems of nine lines each, twenty-four of which are about babies or small children".

Opinions of the Roundel poems move between those who find them captivating and brilliant, to others who find them merely clever and contrived. One of them, A Baby's Death, was set to music by the English composer Sir Edward Elgar as the song "Roundel: The little eyes that never knew Light".

After the first Poems and Ballads, Swinburne's later poetry was devoted more to philosophy and politics, including the unification of Italy, particularly in the volume Songs before Sunrise. He did not stop writing love poetry entirely, indeed it was only in 1882 that his great epic-length poem, Tristram of Lyonesse, was published, its contents lyrical rather than shocking. His versification, and especially his rhyming technique, remain of high quality to the end.

Algernon Charles Swinburne died of influenza, at the Pines in London on April 10th, 1909 at the age of 72. He was buried at St. Boniface Church, Bonchurch on the Isle of Wight.

Algernon Charles Swinburne – A Concise Bibliography

Verse Drama
The Queen Mother (1860)
Rosamond (1860)
Chastelard (1865)
Bothwell (1874)
Mary Stuart (1881)
Marino Faliero (1885)
Locrine (1887)
The Sisters (1892)
Rosamund, Queen of the Lombards (1899)

Poetry
Atalanta in Calydon (1865)*
Poems and Ballads (1866)
Songs Before Sunrise (1871)
Songs of Two Nations (1875)
Erechtheus (1876)*
Poems and Ballads, Second Series (1878)
Songs of the Springtides (1880)
Studies in Song (1880)
The Heptalogia, or the Seven against Sense. A Cap with Seven Bells (1880)
Tristram of Lyonesse (1882)
A Dark Month & Other Poems
A Century of Roundels (1883)
A Midsummer Holiday and Other Poems (1884)
Poems and Ballads, Third Series (1889)
Astrophel and Other Poems (1894)
The Tale of Balen (1896)

A Channel Passage and Other Poems (1904)

*Although formally tragedies, Atlanta in Calydon and Erechtheus are traditionally included with his poetry.

Criticism
William Blake: A Critical Essay (1868, new edition 1906)
Under the Microscope (1872)
George Chapman: A Critical Essay (1875)
Essays and Studies (1875)
A Note on Charlotte Brontë (1877)
A Study of Shakespeare (1880)
A Study of Victor Hugo (1886)
A Study of Ben Johnson (1889)
Studies in Prose and Poetry (1894)
The Age of Shakespeare (1908)
Shakespeare (1909)

Major Collections
The Poems of Algernon Charles Swinburne, 6 vols. 1904.
The Tragedies of Algernon Charles Swinburne, 5 vols. 1905.
The Complete Works of Algernon Charles Swinburne, 20 vols. Bonchurch Edition. 1925-7.
The Swinburne Letters, 6 vols. 1959-62.

www.ingramcontent.com/pod-product-compliance
Lightning Source LLC
Chambersburg PA
CBHW060048050426
42448CB00011B/2356